I0814938

Music Superstars
BAD BUNNY
TORQUE
BY ARIEL FACTOR BIRDOFF
BELLWETHER MEDIA · MINNEAPOLIS, MN

Torque brims with excitement perfect for thrill-seekers of all kinds. Discover daring survival skills, explore uncharted worlds, and marvel at mighty engines and extreme sports. In *Torque* books, anything can happen. Are you ready?

This edition first published in 2025 by Bellwether Media, Inc.

Library of Congress Cataloging-in-Publication Data

Names: Birdoff, Ariel Factor, author.
Title: Bad Bunny / by Ariel Factor Birdoff.
Description: Minneapolis, MN : Bellwether Media, 2025. | Series: Music superstars | Includes bibliographical references and index. | Audience: Ages 7-12 | Audience: Grades 4-6 | Summary: "Engaging images accompany information about Bad Bunny. The combination of high-interest subject matter and light text is intended for students in grades 3 through 7"– Provided by publisher.
Identifiers: LCCN 2024047018 (print) | LCCN 2024047019 (ebook) | ISBN 9798893042603 (library binding) | ISBN 9798893043570 (ebook)
Subjects: LCSH: Bad Bunny, 1994–Juvenile literature. | Singers–Puerto Rico–Biography–Juvenile literature. | Rap musicians–Puerto Rico–Biography–Juvenile literature. | LCGFT: Biographies.
Classification: LCC ML3930.B204 B57 2025 (print) | LCC ML3930.B204 (ebook) | DDC 782.42164092 [B]–dc23/eng/20241008
LC record available at https://lccn.loc.gov/2024047018
LC ebook record available at https://lccn.loc.gov/2024047019

Editor: Elizabeth Neuenfeldt Designer: Josh Brink

Printed in the United States of America, North Mankato, MN.

TABLE OF CONTENTS

ON TOUR!

Lights flash! The crowd cheers! The **orchestra** starts to play. Bad Bunny sings and raps on stage to an excited crowd. He even plays the piano upside down!

THE KING

Bad Bunny is known as the "King of Latin Trap!"

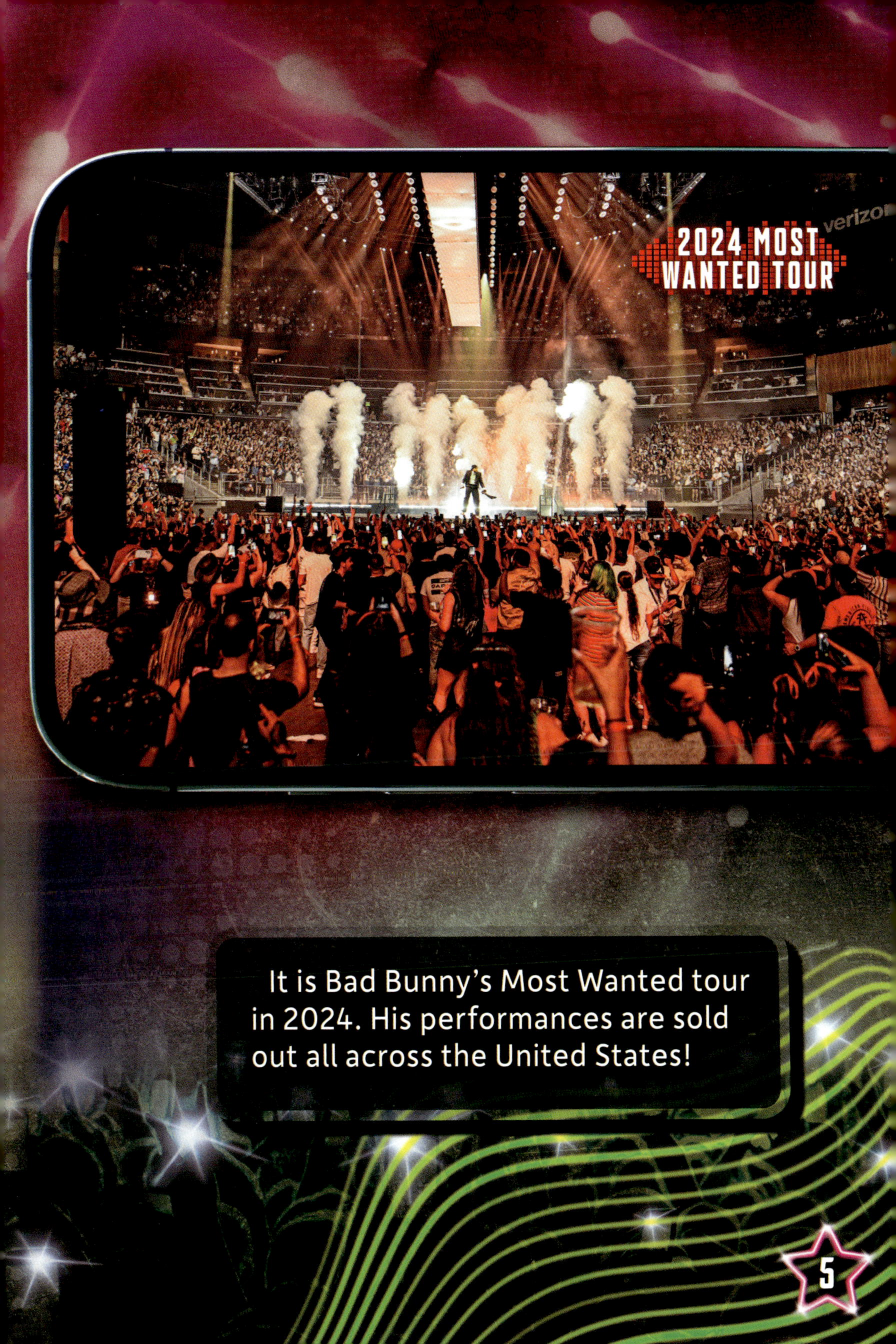

It is Bad Bunny's Most Wanted tour in 2024. His performances are sold out all across the United States!

WHO IS BAD BUNNY?

Benito Antonio Martínez Ocasio, or Bad Bunny, is a Puerto Rican superstar. Bad Bunny is known for his Latin trap and reggaeton music.

BEHIND THE NAME

Bad Bunny got his stage name from a childhood photo of himself looking grumpy and dressed as a bunny!

BAD BUNNY

Birthday	Hometown	Types of Music	First Hit
March 10, 1994	Vega Baja, Puerto Rico	Latin trap, reggaeton	"Soy Peor"

Bad Bunny has five full albums. He has made many singles, too. His popularity has helped spread different types of music to listeners around the world!

A MUSICAL BEGINNING

Bad Bunny grew up in Puerto Rico. He is the oldest of three brothers. His father was a truck driver. His mother was a teacher.

A CHILDHOOD DREAM

Bad Bunny grew up wanting to be a pro wrestler, too. In 2021, he appeared on WWE's WrestleMania! He even jumped off the top rope!

Bad Bunny loved music. His favorite singers were Marc Anthony and Daddy Yankee. When he was 5, Bad Bunny began singing. He wanted to be a performer just like his heroes.

When he was 13, Bad Bunny began writing his own songs. After high school, Bad Bunny studied at the University of Puerto Rico at Arecibo.

FELICIDADES UPRA

UNIVERSITY OF PUERTO RICO AT ARECIBO

FAVORITES

Color
yellow

Food
arroz con salchichas

Accessory
sunglasses

Game
dominoes

While he was there, he continued to make music. He shared it on the internet. DJ Luian, a well-known **producer**, noticed Bad Bunny's music on **SoundCloud**. He signed Bad Bunny to his **record label** in 2016.

PATH TO STARDOM

Bad Bunny first **released** many singles. His first hit "Soy Peor" was **streamed** millions of times.

FOREVER

Bad Bunny's album *X 100PRE* stands for *por siempre* in Spanish. That means "forever" in English.

In 2018, Bad Bunny **collaborated** on a song with Cardi B. It reached number one on the ***Billboard*** Hot 100 chart! Later that year, he released his first album *X 100PRE*. It was a hit!

During the 2020 Super Bowl, Shakira welcomed Bad Bunny as a guest singer during her halftime performance.

Soon after, Bad Bunny released another album called *YHLQMDLG*. This album won Bad Bunny his first **Grammy Award**. It featured many hip-hop and Latin artists. It even featured his childhood hero Daddy Yankee! This was a dream come true!

3 Grammy Awards

6 American Music Awards

15 Latin American Music Awards

11 Latin Grammy Awards

YHLQMDLG

YHLQMDLG is short for *Yo hago lo que me da la gana.* It is Spanish for "I do whatever I want."

In late 2020, Bad Bunny released *El Último Tour del Mundo*. It was the first Spanish-language album to ever hit the *Billboard* 200 chart at number one!

2020 *BILLBOARD* MUSIC AWARDS

In 2022, Bad Bunny won many awards. He won Best Música Urbana Album at the Grammys. He was also named Artist of the Year at the **MTV Video Music Awards**!

Bad Bunny's fourth album, *Un Verano Sin Ti* was released in 2022. It was a huge success! It was number one on the *Billboard* 200 chart. It was the most streamed album on **Spotify** in 2022!

This album was also the first Spanish-language album to be **nominated** for Album of the Year at the Grammys!

TIMELINE

– 2016 –

Bad Bunny signs with the Hear This Music record label

– 2018 –

Bad Bunny releases "I Like It," his first number one song on the *Billboard* Hot 100 chart

2023 GRAMMY AWARDS

– 2022 –

El Último Tour Del Mundo wins Best Música Urbana Album at the Grammys

– 2022 –

Bad Bunny is the first non-English language artist to win the MTV Video Music Award for Artist of the Year

– 2023 –

Un Verano Sin Ti is the first Spanish-language album nominated for Album of the Year at the Grammys

HOPPY FANS!

Bad Bunny has millions of fans. Some fans call themselves *los conejos*. It means "the bunnies." They buy his albums and go to his concerts.

Bad Bunny is a widely loved performer and singing icon. He is an **inspiration** for many budding musicians, just as his heroes were for him!

GLOSSARY

Billboard—related to a well-known music news magazine and website that ranks songs and albums

collaborated—worked with others to create something

Grammy Award—an award given by the Recording Academy of the United States for an achievement in music; Grammy Awards are also called Grammys.

inspiration—someone or something that gives someone an idea about what to do or create

MTV Video Music Awards—yearly awards presented for achievements in music videos, as well as the top songs, artists, and performances

nominated—chosen as a candidate for an award

orchestra—a group of musicians performing instrumental music

producer—a person who takes charge and provides money to make something

record label—a company that sells music

released—made music available for listening

SoundCloud—a streaming platform used for uploading and listening to music, especially from new or independent artists

Spotify—a streaming service that allows people to listen to music, podcasts, and audiobooks

streamed—listened to or played online

TO LEARN MORE

AT THE LIBRARY

Kaplan, Arie. *96 Facts About Bad Bunny*. New York, N.Y.: Grosset & Dunlap, 2024.

Romo Edelman, Claudia, and Ann Dávila Cardinal. *Bad Bunny*. New York, N.Y.: Roaring Brook Press, 2024.

Taboas Zayas, G.M. *Who is Bad Bunny?* New York, N.Y.: Penguin Workshop, 2024.

ON THE WEB

FACTSURFER

Factsurfer.com gives you a safe, fun way to find more information.

1. Go to www.factsurfer.com.
2. Enter "Bad Bunny" into the search box and click 🔍.
3. Select your book cover to see a list of related content.

INDEX

The images in this book are reproduced through the courtesy of: Owen Sweeney/ Invision/ AP Newsroom, front cover (Bad Bunny); Catsense, front cover (lights); Taya Ovod, pp. 2-3; Alexander Tamargo/ Getty Images, p. 3; GFR Media/ Nahira Montcourt/ AP Newsroom, p. 4; Paras Griffin/ Getty Images, p. 5; Kristy Sparow/ Stringer/ Getty Images, p. 6; Jordan Strauss/ Invision/ AP Newsroom, p. 7 (infographic); Sipa USA/ Alamy, p. 7; AP Photo/ Dennis M. Rivera Pichardo/ AP Newsroom, p. 8; Ethan Miller/ Getty Images, pp. 8-9, 12; Kako13/ Wikipedia, p. 10; Manny Hernandez/ Getty Images, p. 11 (DJ Luian); Elena11, p. 11 (color); AS Foodstudio, p. 11 (arroz con salchichas); Drozdin Vladimir, p. 11 (sunglasses); New Africa, p. 11 (dominoes); Frederick M. Brown/ Getty Images, p. 13; Anthony Behar/ Sipa USA/ AP Newsroom, p. 14; Kevin Winter/ Getty Images, pp. 14-15; CarlosVdeHabsburgo/ Wikipedia, p. 15 (Grammy Awards); s_bukley, p. 15 (American Music Awards); Kevin Mazur/ Getty Images, pp. 16, 21; Noam Galai/ Stringer/ Getty Images, p. 17; Johnny Nunez/ Getty Images, pp. 18-19; WFDJ_Stock, p. 19 (MTV Video Music Award); Dabarti CGI, pp. 18-19 (timeline mixing board); jbrink, p. 19, 21 (playlist); Marta Lavandier/ AP Newsroom, p. 20 (fans); DFree, p. 23.